WONDER
STARTERS

Birds

Pictures by ESME EVE

Published by WONDER BOOKS
A Division of Grosset & Dunlap, Inc.

51 Madison Avenue   New York, N.Y. 10010

Published in the United States by Wonder Books, a Division
of Grosset & Dunlap, Inc.

ISBN: 0-448-09666-8 (Trade Edition)
ISBN: 0-448-06386-7 (Library Edition)

FIRST PRINTING 1973

Printed and bound in the United States.

Library of Congress Catalog Card Number: 73-1970

I'm feeding the birds.
The birds are tame.

beak

feet

wing

tail

One bird flies away.
It flaps its wings.
2

A bird lands on my hand.
It puts out its feet.
Its tail feathers help it to stop.

3

Birds with long wings
can glide.
They move their wings slowly.

4

Many sea birds are good gliders.
They watch for fish in the sea.
They dive down very fast.

5

Hawks glide.
They look for little animals.
They dive down and catch the animals
with their claws.
6

Once people kept tame falcons.
Falcons hunted little birds and animals.
Falcons have sharp claws.
So people had to wear gloves.

7

Some people race tame pigeons.
Men take them far from home.
The birds race
all the way home.

8

Swallows migrate.
They fly to a warm place
for the winter.
They fly back again for the summer.

9

Geese and ducks are water birds.
They have webbed feet.
Webbed feet are good for swimming.

Some birds wade in water.
They have long legs and long beaks.
They pull worms out of the mud.

Different birds eat different food.
They need different beaks.

Woodpeckers have very sharp beaks.
They peck holes in wood.
They find insects to eat.

Most birds make nests.
Hen birds lay eggs in nests.
They sit on the eggs
to keep them warm.
14

Soon the baby birds hatch.
Birds bring food
to their babies.

Some birds are very beautiful.
Peacocks have long feathers.
This king kept tame peacocks.
16

Some people keep tame parrots.
Parrots can learn to
say words.

Some birds are good to eat.
People eat chickens
and turkeys and ducks.

Some people shoot birds.
These men are shooting ducks.
A dog brings the
birds back to the men.

Long ago there were flying
animals like this.
Now there are none left.

This bird was called a Dodo.
There are no Dodos left now.

See for yourself.
Put out some fruit.
Which birds eat fruit?
Put out some nuts.
Which birds eat nuts?
22

Starter's **Birds** words

wing
(page 2)

eet
(page 2)

tail
(page 2)

feather
(page 2)

sea bird
(page 5)

dive
(page 5)

hawk
(page 6)

claw
(page 6)

pigeon
(page 8)

swallow
(page 9)

23

goose
(page 10)

duck
(page 10)

webbed foot
(page 10)

wade
(page 11)

beak
(page 11)

woodpecker
(page 13)

insects
(page 13)

nest
(page 14)

eggs
(page 14)

sit
(page 14)

24

peacock
(page 16)

shoot
(page 19)

parrot
(page 17)

Dodo
(page 21)

chicken
(page 18)

fruit
(page 22)

turkey
(page 18)

nuts
(page 22)